THE ULTIMATE GUIDE TO SELLING ON ETSY

How to Sell on Etsy, 100+ Product Ideas, and Best Selling Advice

Genevieve Velzian

Copyright © 2024 Genevieve Velzian

All rights reserved

Any similarity to real persons, living or dead, is coincidental and not intended by the author. All recommendations and opinions are the author's own and are subjective. The author accepts no liability for advice given.

No part of this book may be reproduced, or stored in a retrieval system, or transmitted in any form or by any means, electronic, mechanical, photocopying, recording, or otherwise, without express written permission of the publisher.

INTRODUCTION TO ETSY

Overview of Etsy

Etsy is a unique online marketplace that has carved a niche for itself by focusing on handmade, vintage, and craft supply items. Founded in 2005, Etsy has grown exponentially, attracting millions of buyers and sellers from around the globe.

Unlike generic e-commerce platforms, Etsy emphasises creativity, individuality, and artisanal craftsmanship, making it an ideal marketplace for creative entrepreneurs.

This chapter will introduce you to Etsy, explain why it's a compelling choice for selling your products, and set the stage for your journey as an Etsy seller.

Why Sell on Etsy?

1. A Targeted Audience:

Etsy's user base consists of people specifically looking for unique, handmade, or vintage items. This means that your products are likely to reach a more interested and engaged audience than on broader e-commerce platforms.

2. Built-in Community:
Etsy fosters a sense of community among buyers and sellers. This community aspect not only encourages repeat business but also provides a supportive network where sellers can share advice, experiences, and tips.

3. Ease of Use:
Setting up a shop on Etsy is straightforward, even for those new to e-commerce. The platform provides step-by-step guides and resources to help you get started and grow your business.

4. SEO and Marketing Tools:
Etsy offers various tools to help improve your shop's visibility in search results, both within Etsy and on external search engines. These include keyword optimization, promoted listings, and social media integration.

5. Cost-Effective:
Etsy's fees are relatively low compared to other e-commerce platforms. With a small listing fee and a reasonable commission on sales, it's a cost-effective way to start and maintain an online store.

Understanding the Etsy Community

Etsy's community is diverse but united by a common interest in unique and creative products. Understanding the demographics and behavior of Etsy's audience can help you tailor your products and marketing strategies more effectively.

1. Demographics:
The majority of Etsy buyers are women, often aged between 18 and 35, who value creativity and individuality. However, there's a significant market among older buyers and men as well, especially in categories like vintage items and handmade crafts.

2. Buyer Behavior:
Etsy buyers are often looking for personalized, custom-made items. They appreciate the story behind the products and the artisans who make them. Highlighting the craftsmanship and uniqueness of your items can attract more buyers.

3. Community Engagement:
Etsy encourages interaction between buyers and sellers through reviews, messages, and shop updates. Engaging with your customers can build loyalty and encourage positive reviews, which are crucial for your shop's reputation and success.

Setting Expectations

Starting an Etsy shop is exciting, but it's important to set realistic expectations about the time and effort required. Here are a few key points to consider:

1. Time Commitment:
Running a successful Etsy shop involves more than just creating products. You'll need to invest time in marketing, customer service, order fulfillment, and shop management. Many sellers start part-time but be prepared for the commitment it requires.

2. Learning Curve:
There's a learning curve to understanding Etsy's platform, SEO best practices, and effective marketing strategies. Take advantage of Etsy's resources and community forums to learn and grow.

3. Initial Investment:
While Etsy is cost-effective, there will still be some initial investments needed for materials, branding, and possibly advertising. Budget accordingly and track your expenses.

4. Patience and Perseverance:
Building a successful Etsy shop doesn't happen overnight. It requires patience, perseverance, and continuous improvement. Celebrate small milestones and keep refining your approach based on what works and what doesn't.

By understanding what Etsy offers, recognising its audience, and setting realistic expectations, you're laying a strong foundation for your journey.

In the next chapter, we'll dive into the practical steps of setting up your Etsy shop, from creating an account to crafting your brand identity. Whether you're a seasoned seller or a complete beginner, this guide will equip you with the knowledge and tools you need to thrive on Etsy.

SETTING UP YOUR ETSY SHOP

Creating an Account

Starting your journey on Etsy begins with creating an account. Follow these simple steps to set up your shop:

Sign Up: Go to Etsy's homepage and click on "Sell on Etsy" at the top of the page. You'll be prompted to create an account if you don't already have one.

Personal Information: Fill in your details, including your name, email address, and a password. You can also sign up using Google, Facebook, or Apple.

Verification: Verify your email address by clicking on the link sent to your inbox. This step ensures your account is secure and ready for use.

Shop Name and Branding

Choosing a memorable and meaningful name for your shop is crucial. Here's how to make an impact:

Brainstorming: Think about your brand's identity, the products you sell, and the message you want to convey. Write down several potential names.

Uniqueness: Ensure your shop name is unique and not already in use. Etsy will notify you if the name you've chosen is unavailable.

Relevance: Select a name that reflects your products and is easy for customers to remember and search for.

Future-Proofing: Consider the long-term. Choose a name that allows for potential expansion of your product range.

Once you've chosen your shop name, it's time to build your brand identity:

Logo and Visuals: Design a professional logo and select a colour scheme that represents your brand. Consistency in visuals helps build brand recognition.

Voice and Tone: Define the voice and tone of your brand. Are you quirky, professional, vintage, or modern? Your brand's personality should shine through in all communications.

Storytelling: Share your story. Customers on Etsy love to know the story behind the products. Write a compelling "About" section that tells who you are and why you do what you do.

Shop Policies

Clear and fair shop policies build trust with customers and can help avoid misunderstandings. Here's how to set them up:

Shipping: Outline your shipping policies, including processing times, shipping methods, and delivery estimates. Be transparent about any potential delays.

Returns and Exchanges: Clearly state your return and exchange policies. Specify conditions under which returns are accepted, who pays for return shipping, and the timeframe for returns.

Payment Methods: List the payment methods you accept. Etsy Payments is a convenient option that supports various payment methods.

Privacy Policy: Assure customers that their personal information will be kept private and used only for order processing and communication.

Shop Banner and Icon

Visual appeal is key to attracting customers. Your shop banner and icon are the first things visitors will see:

Shop Banner: Create a visually appealing banner that reflects your brand. The recommended size for Etsy banners is 3360 x 840 pixels.

Shop Icon: Design a shop icon that complements your banner and brand. The icon should be 500 x 500 pixels.

Consistency: Ensure your banner and icon are cohesive with your overall brand aesthetics, using the same colours, fonts, and style.

Step-by-Step Guide to Opening Your Shop

With your account, name, branding, and policies ready, it's time to open your shop:

Go to "Sell on Etsy": Click on "Open your Etsy shop" and follow the prompts.

Shop Preferences: Choose your shop language, country, and currency.

Shop Name: Enter the shop name you've chosen.

Stock Your Shop: Add at least one listing. You can add more later, but having a few products listed will make your shop look more appealing from the start.

Payment and Billing: Set up how you'll get paid and enter your billing information.

Review and Launch: Review your shop information to ensure everything is correct, then click "Open Your Shop".

Crafting Your Brand Identity

Brand identity goes beyond a logo and a name. It's about creating a cohesive and recognisable presence that resonates with your target audience:

Tagline: Develop a catchy tagline that summarises your brand's essence.

Photography Style: Choose a consistent photography style for your product images. Whether it's bright and airy or dark and moody, consistency is key.

Packaging: Consider how your products will be packaged. Attractive and thoughtful packaging can enhance the customer experience and encourage repeat business.

By following these steps, you'll lay a solid foundation for your Etsy shop, setting the stage for future success. In the next chapter, we'll dive into product creation and listing, helping you showcase your products in the best possible light.

PRODUCT CREATION AND LISTING

Product Research

Before you start crafting your products, it's essential to conduct thorough product research to ensure there is a demand for what you plan to sell. Here's how to go about it:

Identify Trends: Use tools like Google Trends, Pinterest, and Etsy's own search bar to identify what's currently popular. Look for trending items in your niche and consider how you can incorporate these trends into your own products.

Analyse Competitors: Study your competitors to understand what they're offering, their pricing, and how they're marketing their products. Identify gaps in the market that you can fill.

Customer Feedback: Look at customer reviews and feedback on similar products. What do customers like or dislike? Use this information to refine your product ideas.

Keyword Research: Use tools like EtsyRank or Marmalead to find keywords that customers are searching for. This will help you understand what terms to use in your product titles and descriptions.

Creating Quality Products

Quality is paramount on Etsy, where customers are looking for unique, well-made items. Here are some tips to ensure your products meet high standards:

Materials: Use high-quality materials that are durable and aesthetically pleasing. The quality of your materials will significantly impact the final product.

Craftsmanship: Pay attention to the details in your craftsmanship. Clean, well-finished products will stand out and attract positive reviews.

Innovation: While it's good to follow trends, adding your unique twist can set your products apart. Think about how you can innovate within your niche.

Testing: Test your products thoroughly to ensure they are functional and durable. This is particularly important for items that will be used frequently or have moving parts.

Pricing Strategies

Pricing your products correctly is crucial for attracting customers while ensuring profitability. Here's how to develop an effective pricing strategy:

Cost Calculation: Calculate all costs involved in making your product, including materials, labour, and overheads. Don't forget to factor in Etsy fees and shipping costs.

Market Research: Look at what similar products are being sold for on Etsy and other platforms. This will give you a sense of the market rate.

Profit Margin: Decide on a profit margin that makes your business sustainable. A common approach is to add a 50-100% markup on your total costs.

Perceived Value: Consider the perceived value of your product. Unique, handcrafted items can often be sold at a higher price due to their exclusivity and quality.

Discounts and Sales: Plan for occasional discounts or sales to attract customers. Ensure your pricing allows for this without sacrificing your profit margin.

Writing Compelling Descriptions

A well-crafted product description can make the difference between a casual browser and a committed buyer. Follow these guidelines to write compelling descriptions:

Clear and Concise: Start with a clear, concise description of what the product is and its primary benefits.

Details: Include all relevant details such as size, materials, care instructions, and variations (colours, sizes, etc.).

Storytelling: Tell the story behind your product. How was it made? What inspired it? Personal stories can create a connection with potential buyers.

Keywords: Use relevant keywords naturally within your description to improve search visibility. Avoid keyword stuffing as it can make your description hard to read.

Call to Action: End with a call to action, encouraging customers to purchase or add the item to their favourites.

Photography Tips

High-quality photos are crucial on Etsy, where customers can't physically touch or see the product. Here's how to take great product photos:

Lighting: Use natural light wherever possible. If shooting indoors, position your product near a window and use a reflector to eliminate shadows.

Background: Use a clean, uncluttered background that complements but doesn't distract from your product. White or neutral colours work well.

Angles: Take multiple photos from different angles to show all aspects of your product. Include close-ups to highlight details and textures.

Context: Show your product in context. For example, if you're selling jewellery, include a photo of it being worn. This helps customers visualise how they might use the product.

Consistency: Maintain a consistent style across all your product photos. This helps to create a cohesive look for your shop and reinforces your brand identity.

By conducting thorough product research, creating high-quality items, pricing them correctly, writing compelling descriptions, and taking excellent photos, you'll be well on your way to creating attractive and effective product listings. In the next chapter, we'll explore how to optimise these listings to ensure they reach the widest possible audience on Etsy.

OPTIMISING YOUR LISTINGS

SEO Basics for Etsy

Understanding how Etsy's search algorithm works is key to ensuring your products are easily found by potential customers. Here are some basic principles of Etsy SEO:

Relevance: Etsy's search algorithm prioritises listings that match the keywords entered by a user. Ensure your titles, tags, and descriptions are relevant to what buyers are searching for.

Quality: High-quality listings that receive positive reviews and have high conversion rates are favoured by the algorithm. Ensure your listings are detailed and engaging.

Recency: Newly listed or recently updated items get a temporary boost in search results. Regularly updating your listings can help maintain their visibility.

Customer and Market Experience: Shops with good customer service, favourable reviews, and complete policies are more likely to rank higher.

Keyword Research

Finding the right keywords is crucial for optimising your listings. Here's how to conduct effective keyword research:

Brainstorming: Think like a buyer. What words and phrases would you use to search for your products?

Tools: Use tools like Etsy's search bar, EtsyRank, Marmalead, and Google Keyword Planner to discover popular search terms related to your products.

Long-Tail Keywords: Focus on long-tail keywords, which are more specific phrases that buyers might use. These often have less competition and attract more targeted traffic.

Competitor Analysis: Look at the keywords your successful competitors are using. This can give you insights into what works in your niche.

Tagging and Titles

Effective use of tags and titles can significantly improve your search visibility. Here's how to make the most of them:

Optimised Titles: Your title should be clear, descriptive, and keyword-rich. Include the most important keywords at the beginning of the title, as Etsy gives more weight to the first few words.

Unique and Specific Tags: Use all 13 available tags for each listing. Include a mix of broad and specific keywords to cover various search queries.

Synonyms and Variations: Use synonyms and variations of your main keywords to capture different ways buyers might search for your product.

Seasonal and Trending Keywords: Update your tags to include seasonal keywords (e.g., "Christmas gift") and trending terms to stay relevant.

Product Attributes

Using attributes effectively can enhance your listings' searchability. Here's how to utilise them:

Categories and Subcategories: Choose the most accurate categories and subcategories for your products. This helps Etsy place your items in front of the right audience.

Attributes: Fill out all available attributes (e.g., colour, size, material). These details help your listings appear in relevant searches and filters.

Occasion and Recipient: Specify the occasion (e.g., "Mother's Day", "wedding") and the recipient (e.g., "for him", "for children"). These attributes can help match your products to buyers' needs.

Styles and Variations: Include styles (e.g., "boho", "modern") and variations (e.g., different sizes or colours) to broaden your listing's appeal and visibility.

Updating and Maintaining Listings

Regular updates and maintenance can keep your listings fresh and improve their performance. Here's what to focus on:

Regular Updates: Periodically update your titles, tags, and descriptions with new keywords or changes based on what's performing well.

Monitor Performance: Use Etsy's analytics tools to track which listings are performing well and which aren't. Adjust your SEO strategy accordingly.

Customer Feedback: Pay attention to customer feedback and reviews. Make adjustments to your listings based on common suggestions or issues raised.

Seasonal Adjustments: Update your listings for seasonal trends and holidays. For example, highlight gift items during Christmas or romantic products for Valentine's Day.

Best Practices for Listing Optimisation

Following best practices can ensure your listings are always at their best. Here are some tips:

High-Quality Photos: Ensure your photos are high-quality and accurately represent your product. Include multiple angles and contextual shots.

Compelling Descriptions: Write detailed and engaging descriptions. Tell the story behind your product, highlight its unique features, and use persuasive language.

Competitive Pricing: Ensure your pricing is competitive yet profitable. Monitor competitor pricing and adjust accordingly.

Customer Service: Provide excellent customer service. Respond promptly to inquiries, handle issues professionally, and aim for positive reviews.

By focusing on SEO basics, conducting thorough keyword research, optimising your tags and titles, using attributes effectively, and maintaining your listings, you'll maximise your shop's visibility and attract more customers. In the next chapter, we'll explore various marketing strategies to drive traffic to your Etsy shop and boost your sales.

MARKETING YOUR ETSY SHOP

Social Media Marketing

Social media is a powerful tool for promoting your Etsy shop. Here's how to effectively use different platforms:

Instagram:

Visual Content: Share high-quality images of your products, behind-the-scenes shots, and customer photos. Use Instagram Stories and Reels to engage with your audience.

Hashtags: Use relevant hashtags to increase visibility. Research popular hashtags in your niche and create a branded hashtag for your shop.

Engagement: Engage with your followers by responding to comments, liking their posts, and using interactive features like polls and Q&A sessions.

Pinterest:

Pin Your Products: Create attractive pins for each of your products, linking directly to your Etsy listings. Use high-quality images and descriptive titles.

Boards: Organise your pins into themed boards that reflect your brand and appeal to your target audience.

SEO: Optimise your pins and boards with relevant keywords to improve their visibility in Pinterest searches.

Facebook:

Business Page: Set up a Facebook business page for your shop. Post regularly about new products, promotions, and behind-the-scenes content.

Groups: Join relevant Facebook groups where your target audience is active. Participate in discussions and share your products when appropriate.

Advertising: Use Facebook Ads to target specific demographics and interests. Experiment with different ad formats like carousel ads and video ads.

Twitter:

Regular Updates: Tweet regularly about your products, promotions, and updates. Use relevant hashtags to increase reach.

Engage: Interact with your followers and other users by replying to tweets, retweeting interesting content, and participating in Twitter chats.

Promotions: Share time-sensitive promotions and flash sales to create a sense of urgency.

Content Marketing

Content marketing involves creating valuable content to attract and engage your target audience. Here's how to leverage it:

Blogging:

Start a Blog: Create a blog on your website or a platform like Medium. Write posts related to your products, industry trends, and DIY projects.

SEO: Optimise your blog posts with relevant keywords to attract organic traffic.

Share: Promote your blog posts on social media and include links to your Etsy shop.

Video Content:

YouTube: Start a YouTube channel and create videos showcasing your products, tutorials, and behind-the-scenes content.

Instagram and Facebook: Use Instagram Stories, IGTV, and Facebook Live to share video content directly with your followers.

SEO: Optimise your video titles and descriptions with relevant keywords.

Email Marketing:

Build a List: Collect email addresses from your customers and website visitors. Offer incentives like discounts or free downloads for subscribing.

Regular Newsletters: Send regular newsletters with updates about new products, promotions, and exclusive content.

Personalisation: Personalise your emails by addressing recipients by name and tailoring content to their preferences.

Paid Advertising

Investing in paid advertising can help you reach a larger audience and drive traffic to your Etsy shop. Here's how to get started:

Etsy Ads:

Promoted Listings: Use Etsy Ads to promote your listings within Etsy's search results. Set a daily budget and monitor your campaign's performance.

Targeting: Use Etsy's targeting options to reach specific demographics and interests.

Google Ads:

Search Ads: Create search ads that appear when users search for relevant keywords on Google.

Shopping Ads: Use Google Shopping ads to showcase your products with images, prices, and links to your Etsy shop.

Display Ads: Use display ads to reach users across Google's network of websites and apps.

Social Media Ads:

Facebook and Instagram Ads: Use Facebook Ads Manager to create targeted ads for both Facebook and Instagram. Experiment with different ad formats and targeting options.

Pinterest Ads: Promote your pins to reach a larger audience on Pinterest. Use targeting options to reach users based on their interests and behaviours.

Twitter Ads: Use Twitter Ads to promote your tweets and reach a larger audience. Experiment with different ad formats and targeting options.

Collaborations and Influencer Marketing

Collaborating with other brands and influencers can help you reach new audiences. Here's how to make the most of it:

Brand Collaborations:

Partnerships: Partner with complementary brands for joint promotions, giveaways, and product bundles. This can help you reach each other's audiences.

Co-Create Products: Collaborate on creating unique products that incorporate both brands' aesthetics and appeal to a broader audience.

Influencer Marketing:

Identify Influencers: Look for influencers in your niche with a significant following and high engagement rates.

Outreach: Reach out to influencers with a personalised message, offering to send them your products in exchange for a review or feature.

Sponsored Posts: Consider paying influencers for sponsored posts, where they promote your products to their followers.

Analytics and Adjustment

Regularly analysing your marketing efforts and making necessary adjustments is crucial for success. Here's how to stay on top of it:

Track Performance: Use tools like Google Analytics, Etsy's Shop Manager, and social media insights to track the performance of your marketing campaigns.

Measure ROI: Calculate the return on investment (ROI) for your paid advertising campaigns to ensure they are profitable.

Adjust Strategies: Based on your analysis, adjust your marketing strategies to focus on what works best. Continuously experiment with new tactics and approaches.

By leveraging social media, content marketing, email marketing, paid advertising, and collaborations, you can effectively drive traffic to your Etsy shop and boost your sales. In the next chapter, we'll explore how to provide exceptional customer service and build lasting relationships with your customers.

CUSTOMER SERVICE AND ENGAGEMENT

Communication Tips

Effective communication is essential for building a positive relationship with your customers. Here are some key tips:

Prompt Responses: Aim to respond to customer enquiries within 24 hours. Prompt replies show that you value their time and business.

Professional Tone: Always maintain a professional and courteous tone, even if the customer is upset or difficult.

Clear Information: Provide clear and concise information in your responses. Avoid jargon and ensure your instructions or answers are easy to understand.

Personal Touch: Personalise your messages. Address customers by their name and reference specific details from their query or order.

Templates: Create templates for common questions, but customise them to avoid sounding robotic. This can save time while still offering a personal touch.

Handling Disputes and Returns

Even with the best customer service, disputes and returns are inevitable. Here's how to handle them effectively:

Remain Calm: Stay calm and composed. Take a step back if needed to ensure you respond professionally.

Listen and Empathise: Listen to the customer's concerns and show empathy. Acknowledge their feelings and reassure them that you're there to help.

Find a Solution: Work with the customer to find a satisfactory solution. Whether it's a refund, replacement, or another resolution, aim to leave the customer feeling positive about the outcome.

Clear Policies: Ensure your return and dispute policies are clear and easily accessible. Refer to these policies when addressing issues to maintain consistency.

Learn and Improve: Use feedback from disputes and returns to improve your products and services. Look for patterns in complaints and address the root causes.

Building Customer Loyalty

Loyal customers are more likely to make repeat purchases and recommend your shop to others. Here's how to build and maintain customer loyalty:

Quality Products: Consistently deliver high-quality products that meet or exceed customer expectations.

Exceptional Service: Provide outstanding customer service that makes customers feel valued and appreciated.

Personalisation: Offer personalised recommendations and special offers based on customers' previous purchases and preferences.

Loyalty Programmes: Consider implementing a loyalty programme that rewards repeat customers with discounts, exclusive offers, or early access to new products.

Follow-Up: Follow up with customers after their purchase to ensure they're satisfied and to encourage feedback and reviews.

Utilising Reviews

Positive reviews can significantly impact your shop's reputation and sales. Here's how to encourage and utilise customer reviews:

Request Reviews: Politely ask satisfied customers to leave a review. Include a request in your order confirmation email and follow-up messages.

Make it Easy: Provide clear instructions on how to leave a review. The easier the process, the more likely customers are to do it.

Showcase Reviews: Highlight positive reviews on your shop's homepage, product listings, and social media. This builds trust and credibility with potential buyers.

Respond to Reviews: Respond to reviews, both positive and negative. Thank customers for their positive feedback and address any issues raised in negative reviews professionally and constructively.

Learn from Feedback: Use the feedback from reviews to improve your products and services. Look for recurring themes and make necessary adjustments.

Engaging with Your Customers

Engaging with your customers helps build a strong relationship and fosters a sense of community around your brand. Here's how to keep your customers engaged:

Social Media Interaction: Engage with your followers on social media by liking, commenting, and sharing their posts. Run interactive polls, Q&A sessions, and contests to encourage participation.

Newsletters: Send regular newsletters with updates about new products, upcoming sales, and exclusive content. Personalise the content to make it relevant to each subscriber.

Customer Stories: Feature customer stories and testimonials on your social media and shop page. This not only provides social proof but also makes your customers feel valued.

Behind-the-Scenes Content: Share behind-the-scenes content to give customers a glimpse into your creative process and the story behind your brand.

Special Events: Host special events such as live streams, virtual workshops, or in-person meetups to connect with your customers and create a sense of community.

Handling Negative Feedback

Negative feedback is inevitable, but how you handle it can make a significant difference. Here's how to manage negative feedback effectively:

Stay Calm: Don't take negative feedback personally. Approach it as an opportunity to improve.

Acknowledge and Apologise: Acknowledge the customer's concerns and apologise for any inconvenience caused. A sincere apology can go a long way in diffusing a tense situation.

Investigate the Issue: Look into the issue to understand what went wrong. This helps you address the problem effectively and prevent it from happening again.

Offer a Solution: Propose a fair and reasonable solution to the customer. This could be a refund, replacement, or another form of compensation.

Learn and Improve: Use negative feedback as a learning tool. Make necessary changes to your products, policies, or processes to avoid similar issues in the future.

By providing exceptional customer service, effectively handling disputes and returns, building customer loyalty, utilising reviews, and engaging with your customers, you can create a positive shopping experience that encourages repeat business and word-of-mouth referrals.

In the next chapter, we'll explore how to manage your Etsy shop efficiently, from inventory management to time management strategies.

MANAGING YOUR ETSY SHOP

Inventory Management

Efficient inventory management is crucial for maintaining a smooth-running Etsy shop. Here's how to keep track of your stock and supplies:

Inventory Tracking: Use an inventory management system or software to track your stock levels. This helps you avoid overselling and ensures you have enough materials to fulfil orders.

Organisation: Keep your physical inventory organised. Label storage bins, shelves, and containers clearly, and arrange items in a logical order.

Reorder Points: Set reorder points for your materials and products. When your stock reaches a certain level, it's time to reorder to avoid running out.

Regular Audits: Conduct regular inventory audits to verify stock levels and identify any discrepancies.

This helps you maintain accurate records and catch any issues early.

Supplier Relationships: Build strong relationships with your suppliers. Reliable suppliers can help ensure you receive materials on time and at a consistent quality.

Order Fulfilment

Efficient order fulfilment is essential for customer satisfaction and repeat business. Here's how to streamline your process:

Processing Orders: Process orders promptly. Aim to ship items within the timeframe specified in your shop policies.

Packaging: Use high-quality packaging materials to protect your products during transit. Consider branded packaging to enhance the unboxing experience.

Shipping Labels: Print shipping labels at home to save time. Etsy offers discounted shipping rates and the ability to print labels directly from your shop dashboard.

Tracking: Provide tracking information to customers once their order has shipped. This helps them know when to expect their delivery and reduces the likelihood of inquiries about order status.

International Shipping: Familiarise yourself with international shipping requirements and customs regulations. Ensure your products are properly labelled and all necessary forms are completed to avoid delays.

Time Management

Balancing your Etsy shop with other responsibilities requires effective time management. Here are some strategies to help you stay organised:

Schedule: Create a daily or weekly schedule to allocate specific times for different tasks such as product creation, listing, marketing, and order fulfilment.

Prioritise: Identify your most important tasks and prioritise them. Focus on high-impact activities that contribute to your shop's growth and success.

Batch Processing: Batch similar tasks together to improve efficiency. For example, dedicate specific times for creating products, photographing items, and updating listings.

Delegation: Consider outsourcing or delegating tasks that are time-consuming or outside your expertise. This could include hiring a virtual assistant, a professional photographer, or a social media manager.

Time-Tracking: Use time-tracking tools to monitor how you spend your time. This can help you identify areas where you can improve efficiency and make better use of your time.

Using Etsy Tools

Etsy offers a variety of tools to help you manage your shop more effectively. Here's an overview of some useful features:

Shop Manager: The Shop Manager dashboard provides an overview of your shop's performance, including sales, orders, and traffic. Use this tool to monitor your shop's activity and track your progress.

Stats: The Stats feature offers detailed analytics about your shop's traffic, listing views, and customer behaviour. Use this data to understand what's working and where you can improve.

Shipping Labels: Purchase and print shipping labels directly from Etsy. This feature includes discounted shipping rates and the ability to manage shipments from your dashboard.

Inventory Management: Use the inventory management tools to keep track of your stock levels and manage variations of your products.

Marketing Tools: Etsy offers various marketing tools, including Etsy Ads, social media integration, and the ability to offer discounts and promotions.

Financial Management

Managing your finances effectively is crucial for the sustainability of your Etsy shop. Here are some key aspects to consider:

Budgeting: Create a budget to manage your expenses and ensure you're setting aside enough for materials, marketing, and other costs.

Pricing Strategy: Regularly review your pricing strategy to ensure you're covering your costs and making a profit. Factor in Etsy fees, shipping costs, and other expenses.

Bookkeeping: Keep accurate financial records of your income and expenses. Use accounting software or hire a bookkeeper to help manage your finances.

Taxes: Understand your tax obligations as an Etsy seller. Keep detailed records of your sales and expenses, and consult with a tax professional to ensure you're compliant with local regulations.

Savings and Investments: Set aside a portion of your profits for savings and reinvestment in your business. This can help you grow and scale your shop over time.

Handling Growth

As your Etsy shop grows, you may face new challenges and opportunities. Here's how to handle growth effectively:

Scaling Production: As demand increases, consider ways to scale your production. This could include hiring additional staff, outsourcing parts of the production process, or investing in equipment to increase efficiency.

Expanding Product Lines: Introduce new products or variations to keep your shop fresh and attract repeat customers. Conduct market research to identify new opportunities.

Wholesale and Bulk Orders: Explore opportunities for wholesale and bulk orders. This can provide a steady stream of income and help you reach new markets.

Time Management: As your shop grows, effective time management becomes even more critical. Continuously refine your processes and delegate tasks to maintain a healthy work-life balance.

Customer Service: Maintain high standards of customer service as your shop grows. Ensure you have systems in place to handle increased customer inquiries and orders efficiently.

By managing your inventory, streamlining order fulfilment, effectively managing your time, utilising Etsy's tools, maintaining financial health, and planning for growth, you can ensure your Etsy shop runs smoothly and sustainably. In the next chapter, we'll explore strategies for scaling your business, including expanding product lines and entering new markets.

SCALING YOUR BUSINESS

Expanding Product Lines

Diversifying your product offerings can attract new customers and increase sales. Here's how to effectively expand your product lines:

Market Research: Conduct market research to identify trends and customer needs. Look for gaps in the market that you can fill with new products.

Customer Feedback: Use feedback from your existing customers to inform your new product ideas. Ask them what they'd like to see in your shop.

Testing New Products: Introduce new products gradually. Start with a small batch to test the market response before committing to larger quantities.

Complementary Products: Consider adding products that complement your current offerings. For example, if you sell handmade jewellery, you could add jewellery boxes or cleaning kits.

Seasonal Items: Introduce seasonal items to capitalise on holidays and special occasions. Plan ahead so you have enough time to create and market these products.

Hiring Help

As your business grows, you may need to hire additional help to manage the increased workload. Here's how to approach hiring:

Identify Needs: Determine which areas of your business require additional support. This could include production, marketing, customer service, or administrative tasks.

Job Descriptions: Write clear job descriptions outlining the responsibilities and qualifications required for each role.

Hiring Process: Develop a structured hiring process, including interviews and trial periods, to ensure you find the right fit for your team.

Training: Provide comprehensive training to ensure new hires understand your processes and standards. This will help maintain the quality and consistency of your products and services.

Outsourcing: Consider outsourcing tasks that don't require a full-time employee. For example, you could hire a freelance graphic designer or a virtual assistant.

Wholesale and Bulk Orders

Expanding into wholesale and bulk orders can provide a steady stream of income and increase your brand's reach. Here's how to get started:

Wholesale Pricing: Develop a wholesale pricing structure that allows for volume discounts while still maintaining profitability. Consider the costs of production, packaging, and shipping.

Minimum Orders: Set minimum order quantities to ensure wholesale orders are worth the effort and resources.

Wholesale Platforms: List your products on wholesale platforms such as Etsy Wholesale, Faire, or Abound to reach potential buyers.

Trade Shows: Participate in trade shows and craft fairs to showcase your products to retailers and bulk buyers.

Marketing Materials: Create professional marketing materials, including a wholesale catalogue and order forms, to present to potential buyers.

International Shipping

Expanding your business internationally can open up new markets and increase sales. Here's how to navigate international shipping:

Shipping Rates: Research and establish competitive shipping rates for international orders. Consider offering flat rates or free shipping thresholds to attract buyers.

Customs and Duties: Understand the customs regulations and duties for different countries. Clearly communicate any potential additional costs to your customers to avoid surprises.

Shipping Partners: Partner with reliable shipping carriers that offer international services. Consider using Etsy's shipping labels to access discounted rates.

Packaging: Ensure your packaging is robust enough to withstand international shipping. Use protective materials and secure packaging methods.

Delivery Times: Provide accurate delivery time estimates for international orders. Keep customers informed about potential delays due to customs or other factors.

Time Management for Growth

Effective time management becomes even more critical as your business grows. Here's how to stay organised and efficient:

Prioritise Tasks: Focus on high-priority tasks that directly impact your business's growth and profitability.

Delegate: Delegate tasks to your team or outsource to free up your time for strategic planning and business development.

Automation: Use automation tools for repetitive tasks such as email marketing, social media scheduling, and order processing.

Scheduling: Create a detailed schedule to allocate time for different aspects of your business. Stick to your schedule to maintain a balanced workload.

Review and Adjust: Regularly review your time management strategies and adjust as needed to accommodate changes in your business.

Financial Planning for Expansion

Effective financial planning is essential for sustainable growth. Here's how to manage your finances as you scale your business:

Budgeting: Create a detailed budget that includes projected income and expenses. Monitor your budget regularly to ensure you're on track.

Cash Flow Management: Maintain a healthy cash flow by managing your receivables and payables efficiently. Consider using accounting software to keep track of your finances.

Funding Options: Explore funding options such as business loans, grants, or investors if you need additional capital for expansion.

Expense Management: Keep a close eye on your expenses and look for ways to reduce costs without compromising quality.

Financial Goals: Set clear financial goals for your business and develop a plan to achieve them. Regularly review your progress and make adjustments as needed.

Maintaining Quality and Consistency

As you scale your business, maintaining the quality and consistency of your products and services is crucial. Here's how to ensure high standards:

Quality Control: Implement strict quality control measures at every stage of production. Regularly inspect materials and finished products to ensure they meet your standards.

Standard Operating Procedures: Develop standard operating procedures (SOPs) for your processes. This ensures consistency and helps train new team members.

Customer Feedback: Continuously gather and analyse customer feedback to identify areas for improvement. Make necessary adjustments to maintain high customer satisfaction.

Supplier Relationships: Maintain strong relationships with your suppliers to ensure you receive high-quality materials consistently.

Brand Consistency: Ensure your branding remains consistent across all platforms and products. This includes your logo, packaging, marketing materials, and customer communications.

By expanding your product lines, hiring help, exploring wholesale and bulk orders, navigating international shipping, managing your time effectively, planning your finances, and maintaining quality and consistency, you can successfully scale your Etsy business. In the next chapter, we'll discuss financial management in more detail, including budgeting, taxes, and record-keeping.

FINANCIAL MANAGEMENT

Budgeting and Planning

Effective budgeting and financial planning are crucial for the sustainability and growth of your Etsy business. Here's how to manage your budget:

Income Projections: Estimate your expected income based on past sales data, market trends, and promotional plans. Be realistic in your projections.

Expense Tracking: List all your business expenses, including materials, shipping, marketing, Etsy fees, and other operational costs. Track these expenses regularly to avoid overspending.

Monthly Budget: Create a monthly budget to manage your cash flow. Allocate funds for each category of expenses and monitor your spending against this budget.

Contingency Fund: Set aside a contingency fund for unexpected expenses or emergencies. This can help you manage unforeseen financial challenges without disrupting your operations.

Review and Adjust: Regularly review your budget and adjust it based on your business performance and any changes in expenses or income.

Taxes and Legal Considerations

Understanding and fulfilling your tax obligations is essential to avoid legal issues and penalties. Here's what you need to know:

Register Your Business: Depending on your location, you may need to register your Etsy shop as a business. Check local regulations and ensure you comply with them.

Sales Tax: Determine if you need to collect sales tax on your sales. Etsy provides tools to help with sales tax collection in the United States, but you'll need to research requirements for other regions.

Income Tax: Keep detailed records of your income and expenses to accurately report your earnings. Consult a tax professional to understand your tax obligations and maximise deductions.

VAT and Import Duties: If you sell internationally, be aware of value-added tax (VAT) and import duties that may apply. Ensure you comply with these regulations to avoid issues with customs.

Record Keeping: Maintain accurate financial records, including sales receipts, expense invoices, and bank statements. This will help you prepare for tax season and any potential audits.

Record Keeping

Keeping detailed and organised financial records is crucial for managing your business effectively. Here's how to maintain your records:

Accounting Software: Use accounting software to track your income, expenses, and other financial transactions. This can simplify record-keeping and make it easier to generate financial reports.

Invoices and Receipts: Keep digital or physical copies of all invoices and receipts. Organise them by category and date for easy reference.

Bank Statements: Regularly reconcile your bank statements with your financial records to ensure accuracy and identify any discrepancies.

Inventory Records: Maintain records of your inventory, including purchases, sales, and stock levels. This helps you manage your stock and calculate the cost of goods sold.

Financial Reports: Generate regular financial reports, such as profit and loss statements, balance sheets, and cash flow statements. These reports provide insights into your business's financial health.

Funding Your Growth

As your business grows, you may need additional funds to expand. Here are some options for financing your growth:

Personal Savings: Use personal savings to fund your business expansion. This can be a low-risk option if you have sufficient savings set aside.

Business Loans: Apply for a business loan from a bank or online lender. Ensure you understand the terms and interest rates before committing.

Grants: Research and apply for business grants that are available to small businesses and entrepreneurs. These grants can provide funding without the need for repayment.

Investors: Seek out investors who are interested in supporting your business. Be prepared to offer a share of your business in exchange for their investment.

Crowdfunding: Use crowdfunding platforms to raise funds from supporters and customers. This can also help you build a community around your brand.

Managing Expenses

Keeping your expenses under control is vital for maintaining profitability. Here's how to manage your expenses effectively:

Cost Analysis: Regularly analyse your expenses to identify areas where you can cut costs. Look for cheaper suppliers, reduce waste, and streamline your operations.

Bulk Purchasing: Buy materials in bulk to take advantage of discounts. Ensure you have adequate storage space and that the materials have a long shelf life.

Outsource Wisely: While outsourcing can save time, it's important to evaluate the cost-effectiveness. Compare the costs of outsourcing versus doing tasks in-house.

Marketing Spend: Track the return on investment (ROI) for your marketing activities. Focus on strategies that deliver the best results and eliminate those that don't.

Overhead Costs: Keep your overhead costs, such as rent and utilities, as low as possible. Consider working from home or sharing a workspace to save on expenses.

Planning for Future Growth

Strategic financial planning is essential for the long-term success of your Etsy business. Here's how to plan for future growth:

Set Financial Goals: Define clear financial goals for your business, such as increasing revenue, reducing costs, or achieving a certain profit margin.

Growth Strategies: Develop strategies to achieve your financial goals. This could include expanding your product line, entering new markets, or increasing your marketing efforts.

Investment in Tools: Invest in tools and technology that can help you grow your business. This could include upgrading your equipment, investing in a new website, or purchasing software to improve efficiency.

Education and Training: Invest in your own education and training to stay updated on industry trends and improve your business skills.

Regular Review: Regularly review your financial plans and adjust them based on your business performance and changes in the market.

By effectively managing your finances, understanding your tax obligations, keeping accurate records, securing funding, controlling expenses, and planning for future growth, you can ensure the financial health and sustainability of your Etsy business. In the next chapter, we'll explore strategies for staying ahead of the curve, including continuous learning, networking, and innovation.

STAYING AHEAD OF THE CURVE

Continuous Learning

To maintain and grow your Etsy business, it's crucial to stay informed about industry trends, new tools, and best practices. Here are some strategies for continuous learning:

Etsy Resources: Regularly visit Etsy's Seller Handbook, forums, and webinars. These resources provide valuable information on the latest features, trends, and tips from successful sellers.

Online Courses: Enrol in online courses related to e-commerce, digital marketing, and business management. Platforms like Coursera, Udemy, and LinkedIn Learning offer a wide range of courses tailored to your needs.

Books and Publications: Read books and industry publications about e-commerce, entrepreneurship, and marketing. Stay updated with new releases to gain fresh perspectives and insights.

Podcasts and Webinars: Listen to podcasts and attend webinars hosted by industry experts. These formats can provide actionable advice and inspiration while fitting into a busy schedule.

Experimentation: Never stop experimenting with new techniques and strategies. Test different approaches to see what works best for your shop and be willing to pivot based on the results.

Networking

Building a network of fellow sellers, customers, and industry professionals can provide support, inspiration, and opportunities for growth. Here's how to effectively network:

Join Etsy Teams: Participate in Etsy Teams related to your niche. These groups offer a platform for discussion, advice, and collaboration with other sellers.

Attend Events: Attend craft fairs, trade shows, and industry conferences. These events provide opportunities to meet other sellers, potential customers, and industry influencers.

Online Communities: Join online communities and forums outside of Etsy, such as Reddit, Facebook groups, and niche-specific forums. Engage in discussions and share your experiences.

Collaborate with Other Sellers: Partner with other Etsy sellers for joint promotions, giveaways, or product collaborations. This can help you reach new audiences and build lasting relationships.

Networking Sites: Use professional networking sites like LinkedIn to connect with industry professionals, join relevant groups, and participate in discussions.

Innovation

Innovation is key to staying competitive and keeping your shop fresh and appealing. Here's how to foster innovation in your business:

Customer Feedback: Listen to your customers' feedback and suggestions. They can provide valuable insights into what they want and how you can improve your products and services.

Trend Analysis: Keep an eye on industry trends and emerging markets. Adapt your products and strategies to align with these trends while maintaining your unique brand identity.

Product Development: Regularly introduce new products and variations. Innovate by incorporating new materials, techniques, or designs to keep your offerings fresh and exciting.

Process Improvement: Continuously look for ways to improve your business processes. This could include adopting new tools, automating tasks, or streamlining production methods.

Creative Thinking: Encourage creative thinking within your team. Foster an environment where new ideas are welcomed and tested, and don't be afraid to take calculated risks.

Future Trends

Staying ahead of future trends can give you a competitive edge. Here are some trends to watch in the e-commerce and Etsy landscape:

Sustainability: As consumers become more eco-conscious, sustainability is increasingly important. Incorporate sustainable practices in your production and packaging, and highlight these efforts in your marketing.

Personalisation: Personalised products are highly sought after. Offer customisation options to cater to this growing demand and make your products stand out.

Social Commerce: Social media platforms are becoming shopping destinations. Leverage features like Instagram Shopping, Facebook Shops, and Pinterest Buyable Pins to sell directly through social media.

Augmented Reality (AR): AR is transforming the online shopping experience. Consider how you can use AR to enhance product visualisation, such as virtual try-ons or home decor previews.

Subscription Models: Subscription boxes and recurring purchase models are gaining popularity. Explore offering subscription services for your products to create a steady revenue stream.

Embracing Technology

Adopting new technologies can streamline your operations and enhance your customer experience. Here's how to integrate technology into your business:

E-commerce Tools: Use e-commerce tools and software to manage your shop more efficiently. This includes inventory management, order processing, and customer relationship management (CRM) systems.

Marketing Automation: Implement marketing automation tools to streamline your email campaigns, social media posts, and ad management. This can save time and ensure consistent communication.

Data Analytics: Leverage data analytics to gain insights into customer behaviour, sales trends, and marketing performance. Use these insights to make informed decisions and optimise your strategies.

Mobile Optimisation: Ensure your Etsy shop and website are optimised for mobile devices. A significant portion of online shopping occurs on mobile, so a seamless mobile experience is crucial.

Cybersecurity: Protect your business and customer data by investing in cybersecurity measures. This includes using secure payment gateways, regularly updating software, and educating yourself on best practices.

By committing to continuous learning, networking effectively, fostering innovation, staying ahead of trends, and embracing technology, you can ensure your Etsy business remains competitive and thrives in a constantly evolving market.

ETSY FOR DROPSHIPPING

Understanding Dropshipping on Etsy

Dropshipping is a business model where you sell products to customers without holding any inventory. Instead, when a customer places an order in your Etsy shop, you purchase the item from a third-party supplier who then ships it directly to the customer. This model allows you to offer a wide range of products without the need for storage space or upfront inventory costs.

Benefits of Dropshipping on Etsy

Low Startup Costs: No need to invest in inventory upfront.

Wide Product Range: Ability to offer a diverse range of products without stocking them.

Reduced Risk: Less financial risk as you only purchase products after a customer orders them.

Scalability: Easier to scale your business by adding new products without worrying about inventory management.

Challenges of Dropshipping on Etsy

Supplier Reliability: Dependence on suppliers for product quality and timely shipping.

Lower Profit Margins: Dropshipping typically has lower profit margins compared to traditional retail.

Quality Control: Less control over product quality and packaging.

Shipping Times: Potential for longer shipping times, especially with international suppliers.

Finding Reliable Suppliers

Finding trustworthy suppliers is crucial for a successful dropshipping business. Here are some tips for sourcing suppliers:

Research: Use platforms like AliExpress, Oberlo, and Spocket to find dropshipping suppliers. Look for suppliers with high ratings and positive reviews.

Direct Contact: Reach out to suppliers directly to establish a relationship and discuss your requirements.

Sample Orders: Place sample orders to evaluate the quality of the products and the reliability of the supplier.

Supplier Directories: Use directories like SaleHoo and Worldwide Brands to find vetted suppliers.

Setting Up Your Dropshipping Shop on Etsy

Niche Selection: Choose a niche that you are passionate about and that has a proven demand. This will help you stand out in the competitive Etsy marketplace.

Shop Setup: Follow the standard steps to set up your Etsy shop. Create a memorable shop name, set up your branding, and define your shop policies.

Product Listings: Create detailed and compelling product listings. Include high-quality images provided by your supplier and write thorough descriptions that highlight the benefits and features of the products.

Pricing Strategy: Set competitive prices that cover the cost of the product, shipping, Etsy fees, and still provide a reasonable profit margin. Consider offering free shipping to attract more customers.

Shipping Policies: Clearly state your shipping policies, including estimated delivery times and any potential delays. Be transparent about the shipping origin if your suppliers are based overseas.

Managing Orders and Customer Service

Order Processing: When a customer places an order, promptly purchase the item from your supplier and provide them with the customer's shipping details. Automate this process using dropshipping tools like Oberlo or Spocket if possible.

Communication: Keep your customers informed throughout the order process. Send order confirmations, shipping notifications, and follow-up messages to ensure a positive buying experience.

Handling Returns: Establish a clear return policy and communicate it to both your customers and suppliers. Coordinate with your suppliers to manage returns and refunds smoothly.

Customer Support: Provide excellent customer service by responding to inquiries quickly and resolving issues efficiently. Build a reputation for reliability and trustworthiness.

Marketing Your Dropshipping Shop

SEO Optimisation: Optimise your product listings with relevant keywords to improve search visibility on Etsy. Use keywords in titles, tags, and descriptions.

Social Media Marketing: Promote your products on social media platforms like Instagram, Pinterest, and

Facebook. Use engaging content and hashtags to reach a broader audience.

Email Marketing: Build an email list and send regular newsletters with updates, promotions, and new product launches.

Etsy Ads: Use Etsy's advertising platform to promote your listings and drive more traffic to your shop. Experiment with different ad campaigns to find what works best for your products.

Influencer Collaborations: Partner with influencers in your niche to promote your products. This can help you reach a larger and more engaged audience.

Tools and Resources for Dropshipping on Etsy

Dropshipping Tools: Use tools like Oberlo, Spocket, and Printful to automate order processing and manage your dropshipping business efficiently.

Inventory Management: Use inventory management software to keep track of your products and avoid overselling.

Analytics: Use Etsy's analytics tools to monitor your shop's performance and make data-driven decisions.

Supplier Platforms: Platforms like AliExpress, SaleHoo, and Worldwide Brands can help you find reliable suppliers.

Educational Resources: Enrol in online courses and read books about dropshipping and e-commerce to continuously improve your skills and knowledge.

Best Practices for Success

Product Selection: Choose products that have high demand, low competition, and good profit margins.

Supplier Relationships: Build strong relationships with your suppliers to ensure reliability and quality.

Customer Experience: Focus on providing an excellent customer experience to build trust and encourage repeat business.

Continuous Improvement: Regularly review your shop's performance and make adjustments to improve your listings, marketing strategies, and customer service.

Legal Considerations: Ensure you comply with all legal requirements, including tax obligations and import/export regulations.

Conclusion

Dropshipping on Etsy can be a lucrative and low-risk way to start an e-commerce business. By finding reliable suppliers, setting up a professional shop, managing orders efficiently, and marketing your products effectively, you can build a successful dropshipping business on Etsy. Remember to continuously learn and adapt to stay ahead of the competition and meet the evolving needs of your customers.

SUCCESS STORIES AND CASE STUDIES

Interviews with Top Sellers

Learning from successful Etsy sellers can provide valuable insights and inspiration for your own business. Here are some key takeaways from interviews with top Etsy sellers:

Sarah's Handmade Jewellery:

Background: Sarah started her Etsy shop as a side hustle while working a full-time job. Her passion for jewellery making quickly turned into a thriving business.

Key Strategies: Sarah focused on high-quality photography and detailed product descriptions. She also invested in social media marketing, particularly Instagram, to showcase her work and connect with potential customers.

Challenges and Solutions: One of her main challenges was managing time effectively. She overcame this by creating a strict schedule and gradually transitioning to full-time work on her Etsy shop.

Advice: Sarah advises new sellers to focus on their unique selling points and to engage actively with their customers through personalised messages and social media.

Tom's Vintage Finds:

Background: Tom has always been passionate about vintage items. He started his Etsy shop to share his unique finds with a broader audience.

Key Strategies: Tom emphasised the importance of niche marketing. By targeting vintage enthusiasts and participating in vintage-related forums and groups, he built a loyal customer base.

Challenges and Solutions: Shipping fragile items was a significant challenge. Tom invested in high-quality packaging materials and developed a meticulous packing process to ensure his products arrived safely.

Advice: Tom suggests new sellers should continuously educate themselves about their niche and build a strong brand identity that resonates with their target audience.

Emily's Custom Stationery:

Background: Emily started her Etsy shop to share her love for custom stationery and paper goods. Her shop quickly gained popularity due to her unique designs and attention to detail.

Key Strategies: Emily focused on personalisation, offering customisation options for most of her products. She also leveraged Etsy Ads to increase her shop's visibility.

Challenges and Solutions: Managing a high volume of custom orders was challenging. Emily streamlined her process by creating templates and standardising parts of the customisation process.

Advice: Emily advises new sellers to be flexible and adaptable, and to always listen to customer feedback to improve their products and services.

Case Studies

Examining detailed case studies can provide deeper insights into the strategies and practices that lead to success. Here are some illustrative case studies:

Case Study: The Rise of Eco-Friendly Home Goods

Shop Overview: GreenLiving is an Etsy shop that sells eco-friendly home goods, including reusable kitchen items, biodegradable cleaning supplies, and sustainable decor.

Strategy: The shop capitalised on the growing trend of sustainability. They used keywords related to eco-friendly living and highlighted the environmental benefits of their products in descriptions and marketing materials.

Marketing Approach: GreenLiving invested heavily in content marketing, creating a blog that offered tips for sustainable living. They also collaborated with eco-conscious influencers to promote their products.

Results: The shop saw a 150% increase in sales over two years, with a significant portion of revenue coming from repeat customers.

Lessons Learned: Emphasising the unique benefits of your products and aligning them with current trends can significantly boost your visibility and sales.

Case Study: Scaling Handmade Clothing

Shop Overview: ArtisanThreads is a shop that specialises in handmade, custom-fit clothing. The shop started as a small operation but has grown significantly over the years.

Strategy: ArtisanThreads focused on high-quality materials and craftsmanship. They offered custom sizing and tailoring, which set them apart from mass-produced clothing brands.

Operational Changes: To scale their business, they invested in better equipment and hired skilled seamstresses. They also implemented a robust inventory management system to keep track of materials and orders.

Results: The shop's revenue tripled in three years, and they expanded their product line to include seasonal collections.

Lessons Learned: Investing in quality and scaling operations methodically can lead to substantial growth without compromising on product standards.

Case Study: Leveraging Seasonal Trends

Shop Overview: FestiveFlares specialises in holiday and seasonal decorations. Their product line changes with each major holiday, offering themed decorations and gifts.

Strategy: FestiveFlares capitalised on seasonal demand by planning their product releases well in advance. They used social media to build anticipation and offered early bird discounts to boost pre-season sales.

Marketing Approach: They created limited-time offers and flash sales during peak seasons, which helped drive urgency and increase sales.

Results: The shop experienced peak sales during holiday seasons, with a 200% increase in sales during the fourth quarter compared to the rest of the year.

Lessons Learned: Leveraging seasonal trends and creating a sense of urgency can significantly boost sales during peak times.

Lessons Learned

From these success stories and case studies, several key lessons emerge:

Quality Matters: High-quality products and attention to detail are essential for building a loyal customer base and receiving positive reviews.

Niche Marketing: Focusing on a specific niche can help you stand out in a crowded marketplace and attract a dedicated audience.

Customer Engagement: Engaging with your customers through personalised messages, social media, and excellent customer service can foster loyalty and repeat business.

Adaptability: Being flexible and willing to adapt your strategies based on customer feedback and market trends is crucial for long-term success.

Planning and Organisation: Proper planning, especially for seasonal trends and scaling operations, can help you manage growth effectively and sustain your business over time.

By learning from the experiences of successful Etsy sellers, you can apply these insights and strategies to your own business, helping you overcome challenges and achieve your goals. In the final chapter, we'll provide a summary of key points, create a personalised action plan, and offer additional resources for further learning and growth.

CONCLUSION AND NEXT STEPS

Summary of Key Points

As we conclude "The Ultimate Guide to Selling on Etsy," let's summarise the key points covered throughout the book:

Introduction to Etsy: We explored what makes Etsy unique and why it's an ideal platform for creative entrepreneurs. Understanding Etsy's community and setting realistic expectations is crucial for new sellers.

Setting Up Your Etsy Shop: Step-by-step guidance on creating your account, choosing a memorable shop name, crafting your brand identity, setting shop policies, and designing your shop's visual appeal.

Product Creation and Listing: Emphasised the importance of quality products, effective pricing strategies, compelling descriptions, and high-quality photography to attract customers.

Optimising Your Listings: Discussed Etsy SEO basics, keyword research, tagging, and utilising product attributes to improve search visibility and attract more buyers.

Marketing Your Etsy Shop: Covered social media marketing, content marketing, email marketing, paid advertising, and collaborations to drive traffic and increase sales.

Customer Service and Engagement: Highlighted the importance of excellent communication, handling disputes professionally, building customer loyalty, utilising reviews, and engaging with your customers.

Managing Your Etsy Shop: Provided strategies for efficient inventory management, order fulfilment, time management, using Etsy tools, and financial management.

Scaling Your Business: Discussed expanding product lines, hiring help, exploring wholesale opportunities, international shipping, and maintaining quality and consistency during growth.

Financial Management: Offered advice on budgeting, tax compliance, record-keeping, funding growth, managing expenses, and planning for future growth.

Staying Ahead of the Curve: Emphasised continuous learning, networking, innovation, future trends, and embracing technology to stay competitive.

Success Stories and Case Studies: Shared insights from successful Etsy sellers and detailed case studies to provide inspiration and practical lessons.

Action Plan

Creating a personalised action plan will help you implement the strategies discussed in this book. Here's a template to get you started:

Set Clear Goals:

Define short-term (3-6 months) and long-term (1-2 years) goals for your Etsy shop.

Examples: Increase monthly sales by 20%, introduce 10 new products, achieve 100 positive reviews.

Research and Planning:

Conduct market research to identify trends and customer needs.

Create a detailed business plan outlining your product range, pricing strategy, marketing plan, and financial projections.

Shop Setup and Optimisation:

Complete your shop setup, ensuring all policies are clear and visuals are appealing.

Optimise your listings with relevant keywords, tags, and high-quality photos.

Marketing and Promotion:

Develop a marketing strategy that includes social media, content marketing, email campaigns, and paid advertising.

Schedule regular posts and promotions to maintain visibility and engagement.

Customer Service Excellence:

Implement best practices for communication and customer service.

Set up systems for managing orders, returns, and feedback efficiently.

Monitor and Adjust:

Regularly review your shop's performance using Etsy's analytics tools.

Adjust your strategies based on data insights and customer feedback.

Continuous Improvement:

Stay updated with Etsy trends and best practices. Invest in learning and networking opportunities to keep your business growing.

Resources and Tools

Here are some additional resources and tools to help you on your Etsy journey:

Etsy Seller Handbook: Comprehensive resource with articles on various aspects of selling on Etsy.

Etsy Forums and Teams: Join communities to connect with other sellers, share experiences, and seek advice.

Online Courses: Platforms like Coursera, Udemy, and LinkedIn Learning offer courses on e-commerce, digital marketing, and business management.

Books: Recommended reads include "Etsy-preneurship" by Jason Malinak, "How to Make Money on Etsy" by Timothy Adam, and "Etsy Empire" by Eric Michael.

Podcasts: Listen to podcasts like "Etsy Conversations," "The Jam by Marmalead," and "Crickets to Cha-Chings" for tips and inspiration.

Accounting Software: Tools like QuickBooks, Xero, and Wave can help you manage your finances efficiently.

Inventory Management: Software like Craftybase, TradeGecko, and Stitch Labs can streamline your inventory processes.

Final Thoughts

Embarking on your Etsy selling journey can be both exciting and challenging. Remember, success on Etsy doesn't happen overnight. It requires patience, dedication, and continuous effort. Here are some final words of wisdom to keep you motivated:

Stay Passionate: Your passion for your products and creativity is what makes your shop unique. Let that passion shine through in everything you do.

Be Resilient: There will be ups and downs. Learn from your setbacks and use them as stepping stones to success.

Focus on Your Customers: Happy customers are the key to a successful Etsy shop. Always strive to exceed their expectations.

Keep Innovating: The e-commerce landscape is constantly evolving. Stay curious, embrace change, and continuously seek new ways to improve and grow your business.

Enjoy the Journey: Selling on Etsy is not just about making money; it's about sharing your creativity with the world. Enjoy the process and celebrate your achievements, big and small.

With the knowledge and strategies provided in this guide, you're well-equipped to build and grow a successful Etsy shop. Best of luck on your journey, and may your creativity and hard work lead you to great success!

BONUS CHAPTER: 100 PRODUCT IDEAS

Finding the perfect product to sell on Etsy can be a challenge, but inspiration can come from many sources. Here's a list of 100 product ideas to spark your creativity and help you find a niche that resonates with Etsy buyers.

Handmade Jewellery

Personalised Name Necklaces: Custom necklaces with names or initials.

Gemstone Rings: Rings featuring various gemstones.

Charm Bracelets: Bracelets with unique charms.

Wire Wrapped Pendants: Artistic pendants made by wrapping wire around stones or crystals.

Handmade Earrings: Earrings crafted from materials like clay, metal, or wood.

Leather Bracelets: Customisable leather bracelets with engravings.

Beaded Necklaces: Colourful, beaded necklaces for various occasions.

Minimalist Jewellery: Simple, elegant pieces for everyday wear.

Home Decor

Decorative Pillows: Customisable throw pillows with unique designs.

Macramé Wall Hangings: Handmade wall decor made from knotted cord.

Hand-Painted Canvases: Original artwork for home decoration.

Wooden Signs: Rustic, personalised wooden signs.

Candles: Scented, handmade candles in various shapes and sizes.

Ceramic Planters: Unique planters for indoor plants.

Wall Decals: Removable wall stickers with various designs.

Woven Baskets: Handcrafted baskets for storage and decoration.

Personalised Gifts

Custom Mugs: Mugs with personalised messages or images.

Photo Albums: Handmade photo albums for special occasions.

Engraved Keychains: Custom keychains with names or messages.

Personalised Notebooks: Notebooks with custom covers or pages.

Custom Phone Cases: Phone cases with personalised designs.

Handwritten Letters: Custom calligraphy for special messages.

Pet Portraits: Custom illustrations of pets.

Personalised T-Shirts: Customisable shirts with names, dates, or designs.

Fashion Accessories

Knitted Scarves: Hand-knitted scarves in various patterns.

Leather Wallets: Handmade wallets with custom engravings.

Headbands: Fabric or knitted headbands for various styles.

Bow Ties: Custom bow ties for special occasions.

Handmade Hats: Unique hats made from various materials.

Reusable Shopping Bags: Eco-friendly, personalised tote bags.

Sunglasses Cases: Customisable cases for eyewear.

Hair Clips and Barrettes: Decorative hair accessories.

Baby and Kids

Handmade Toys: Soft toys made from fabric or yarn.

Personalised Baby Blankets: Customisable baby blankets with names or birth dates.

Children's Clothing: Handmade outfits for babies and toddlers.

Nursery Decor: Wall art, mobiles, and other decorations for nurseries.

Custom Storybooks: Personalised children's books with custom characters.

Teething Rings: Safe, handmade teething rings for babies.

Educational Toys: Handmade toys that help with learning and development.

Baby Booties: Knitted or crocheted booties for infants.

Art and Collectibles

Original Paintings: Unique paintings on canvas or paper.

Prints of Artwork: Reproductions of original artwork.

Handmade Dolls: Collectible dolls with custom outfits.

Vintage Finds: Curated vintage items like jewellery, decor, or clothing.

Sculptures: Handmade sculptures from clay, wood, or metal.

Custom Portraits: Commissioned portraits from photographs.

Handcrafted Journals: Unique journals with custom covers.

Collectible Pins: Enamel pins with various designs.

Beauty and Self-Care

Handmade Soap: Customisable, scented soaps.

Bath Bombs: Colourful, aromatic bath bombs.

Lip Balm: Natural lip balms in various flavours.

Body Scrubs: Exfoliating scrubs made from natural ingredients.

Face Masks: Handmade facial masks for skincare.

Beard Oil: Custom beard oils with various scents.

Lotions and Creams: Handmade lotions for skin care.

Essential Oils: Blended essential oils for aromatherapy.

Wedding and Party

Wedding Invitations: Custom-designed wedding stationery.

Bridal Hair Accessories: Handmade hairpieces for brides.

Party Favors: Unique favours for weddings or parties.

Guest Books: Personalised guest books for weddings.

Table Centerpieces: Handmade decor for event tables.

Wedding Rings: Custom-designed wedding bands.

Save the Dates: Unique cards for announcing wedding dates.

Cake Toppers: Personalised cake decorations.

Office and Stationery

Custom Planners: Personalised planners and organisers.

Desk Accessories: Handmade organisers, pen holders, and other desk items.

Stickers: Customisable stickers for planners or decoration.

Greeting Cards: Handmade cards for various occasions.

Calendars: Personalised wall or desk calendars.

Handmade Pens: Custom pens with unique designs.

Notebook Covers: Handmade covers for notebooks or journals.

Bullet Journals: Customisable journals for bullet journaling.

Outdoor and Garden

Birdhouses: Handmade birdhouses with unique designs.

Garden Markers: Custom plant markers for gardens.

Outdoor Furniture: Handmade benches, tables, or chairs.

Planter Boxes: Wooden planter boxes for gardening.

Wind Chimes: Handmade wind chimes from various materials.

Hammocks: Custom-made hammocks for outdoor relaxation.

Fire Pits: Unique, handcrafted fire pits.

Garden Sculptures: Decorative sculptures for gardens.

Tech Accessories

Laptop Sleeves: Handmade sleeves for laptops.

Cable Organisers: Custom organisers for electronic cables.

Phone Stands: Personalised stands for smartphones.

Tablet Covers: Custom covers for tablets.

Mouse Pads: Unique, handmade mouse pads.

Tech Cleaning Kits: Eco-friendly kits for cleaning electronics.

Headphone Holders: Custom holders for headphones.

Charging Stations: Handmade charging stations for multiple devices.

Seasonal and Holiday

Christmas Ornaments: Handmade ornaments for Christmas trees.

Holiday Wreaths: Customisable wreaths for various holidays.

Halloween Costumes: Handmade costumes for Halloween.

Easter Baskets: Unique baskets for Easter.

Valentine's Gifts: Personalised gifts for Valentine's Day.

Holiday Stockings: Custom Christmas stockings.

Seasonal Decor: Decorations for different seasons.

Advent Calendars: Custom-made advent calendars for Christmas.

Sports and Hobbies

Custom Yoga Mats: Personalised mats for yoga enthusiasts.

Sports Equipment: Handmade gear for various sports.

Hobby Kits: Kits for hobbies like knitting, painting, or model building.

Outdoor Gear: Custom items for camping, hiking, or other outdoor activities.

By exploring these product ideas, you can find a niche that suits your skills and interests, while also appealing to Etsy's unique and diverse customer base. Whether you choose to focus on handmade jewellery, personalised gifts, home decor, or any other category, the key to success is quality, creativity, and a passion for what you create.

PRODUCT EXAMPLES AND TEMPLATES

Crafting compelling product descriptions is essential for attracting customers and converting visits into sales. Here are a few example product descriptions that you can use as templates for different types of products on Etsy.

Template 1: Handmade Jewellery

Product: Personalised Name Necklace

Title: Custom Personalised Name Necklace - Sterling Silver, Gold, or Rose Gold - Perfect Gift for Her

Description:

Discover the perfect blend of elegance and personalisation with our Custom Personalised Name Necklace. This beautiful piece is available in sterling silver, gold, or rose gold, making it a versatile addition to any jewellery collection.

Key Features:

Customisable: Add any name or word of your choice (up to 12 characters).
Material Options: Choose from high-quality sterling silver, 18k gold plating, or rose gold plating.
Chain Length: Available in 16", 18", and 20" lengths to suit your style.

Why You'll Love It:
Whether you're treating yourself or looking for the perfect gift for a loved one, this personalised necklace is a timeless piece that will be cherished for years to come. Each necklace is meticulously crafted to order, ensuring a unique and special touch.

Care Instructions:
To keep your necklace looking its best, avoid exposure to water, perfumes, and lotions. Store it in a cool, dry place when not in use.

Shipping & Delivery:
All items are handmade to order and will be shipped within 5-7 business days. We offer free standard shipping worldwide. Expedited shipping options are available at checkout.

Custom Orders:
Have a special request or need a different length? Feel free to contact us for custom orders. We are happy to accommodate your needs.

Template 2: Home Decor

Product: Macramé Wall Hanging

Title: Large Macramé Wall Hanging - Boho Chic Handmade Home Decor - Perfect for Living Room or Bedroom

Description:
Add a touch of boho chic to your home with our Large Macramé Wall Hanging. Handcrafted with love, this stunning piece is perfect for adding texture and warmth to any space, whether it's your living room, bedroom, or office.

Key Features:

Handmade: Each wall hanging is meticulously handcrafted from high-quality cotton rope.
Dimensions: Measures 30" wide x 40" long, making it a statement piece for any wall.
Design: Features intricate patterns and knots for a unique and artistic look.

Why You'll Love It:
Our macramé wall hanging is not just a decoration, but a piece of art that brings character and personality to your home. The neutral colours blend seamlessly with any decor style, from modern to rustic.

Care Instructions:
To clean, gently shake off any dust or use a soft brush. Avoid direct sunlight to prevent fading.

Shipping & Delivery:
This item is made to order and will be shipped within 10-14 business days. We offer free standard shipping within the US. International shipping is available for an additional fee.

Custom Orders:
Looking for a specific size or colour? Contact us for custom orders. We are happy to create a piece that fits your vision perfectly.

Template 3: Personalised Gifts

Product: Custom Photo Mug

Title: Custom Photo Mug - Personalised Coffee Mug with Your Photo - Perfect Gift for Any Occasion

Description:
Start your day with a smile with our Custom Photo Mug! Personalise this high-quality ceramic mug with your favourite photo, making it a perfect gift for birthdays, anniversaries, or just because.

Key Features:

Personalisation: Add your own photo to create a unique and memorable mug.
Material: Made from durable, high-quality ceramic.
Capacity: Holds 11 oz of your favourite beverage.
Dishwasher & Microwave Safe: Easy to clean and convenient to use.

Why You'll Love It:
Our custom photo mug is a thoughtful and personal gift that's perfect for any occasion. Whether it's a picture of a loved one, a cherished memory, or a fun design, this mug will bring joy with every sip.

How to Order:

Select the quantity and add to cart.
During checkout, upload your high-resolution photo. Please ensure the photo is clear and well-lit for the best results.
Shipping & Delivery:
Your personalised mug will be created and shipped within 3-5 business days. We offer standard and expedited shipping options at checkout.

Custom Orders:
Have a special request or need assistance? Feel free to contact us. We're here to help make your gift perfect.

Template 4: Baby and Kids

Product: Personalised Baby Blanket

Title: Personalised Baby Blanket - Custom Name Blanket - Soft and Cozy for Newborns and Infants

Description:
Wrap your little one in love with our Personalised Baby Blanket. This soft and cozy blanket can be

customised with your baby's name, making it a perfect keepsake for newborns and infants.

Key Features:

Personalisation: Add your baby's name (up to 15 characters) for a special touch.
Material: Made from ultra-soft, hypoallergenic fleece.
Size: Measures 30" x 40", ideal for cribs, strollers, and snuggling.
Design: Choose from a variety of cute and stylish patterns.

Why You'll Love It:
Our personalised baby blanket is not only practical but also a cherished keepsake. It's perfect for baby showers, birthdays, or as a thoughtful gift for new parents.

Care Instructions:
Machine wash cold with like colours. Tumble dry low or lay flat to dry. Do not bleach or iron.

Shipping & Delivery:
This item is custom made to order and will be shipped within 5-7 business days. We offer free standard shipping within the US. International shipping is available at an additional cost.

Custom Orders:
Need a different size or have a special request? Contact us for custom orders. We're happy to create something unique for you.

Template 5: Beauty and Self-Care

Product: Handmade Scented Candle

Title: Handmade Scented Candle - Soy Wax - Relaxing Aromatherapy - Perfect Gift for Any Occasion

Description:
Transform your space with the soothing scents of our Handmade Scented Candle. Made from natural soy wax and infused with essential oils, this candle is perfect for creating a relaxing atmosphere in any room.

Key Features:

Natural Soy Wax: Burns cleanly and evenly, free from harmful chemicals.
Essential Oils: Infused with high-quality essential oils for a calming aroma.
Burn Time: Long-lasting burn time of approximately 40 hours.
Eco-Friendly: Packaged in a recyclable glass jar with a reusable lid.

Scents Available:

Lavender & Vanilla: Relaxing and calming.
Citrus & Sage: Fresh and invigorating.
Rose & Sandalwood: Romantic and warm.

Why You'll Love It:
Our handmade scented candle is perfect for unwinding after a long day, setting the mood for a special occasion, or as a thoughtful gift for a loved one. The natural ingredients ensure a clean burn and a delightful fragrance.

Care Instructions:
Trim the wick to 1/4 inch before each use to ensure a clean burn. Allow the wax to melt to the edges of the jar each time to prevent tunneling.

Shipping & Delivery:
Your candle will be handmade to order and shipped within 3-5 business days. We offer standard and expedited shipping options.

Custom Orders:
Looking for a specific scent or custom label? Contact us for custom orders. We're happy to create a candle that meets your needs.

Using These Templates

To use these templates effectively:

Personalise: Tailor each template to your specific product, including accurate details about materials, sizes, and other unique features.

Highlight Benefits: Focus on what makes your product special and why customers will love it.

Include Keywords: Use relevant keywords naturally throughout the description to improve your product's search visibility.

Call to Action: Encourage customers to make a purchase with clear instructions and incentives.

Professional Photos: Pair your descriptions with high-quality photos to provide a complete and appealing listing.

By using these templates and adapting them to your products, you can create compelling and effective product descriptions that attract customers and drive sales on Etsy.

THE END

ABOUT THE AUTHOR

Genevieve Velzian

Genevieve is a full-time digital nomad, travelling the world and running various online businesses. As well as running a successful Etsy store, Genevieve has a YouTube channel, a dropshipping business, various books, and offers consultancy services to large FMCG brands. Next up in her life plans are starting a podcast and visiting China!

www.ingramcontent.com/pod-product-compliance
Lightning Source LLC
Chambersburg PA
CBHW031441210526
45464CB00005B/2288